Ruby Luna's Curious Journey

Tessa Venuti Sanderson

This book is dedicated to my daughters Zara and Alma, nephew Kit, and all the children who are growing up.

You and your bodies are special. Take care of them and each other.

Hello! I'm Ruby Luna.

My friends and I are going to show you how amazing the female body is.

Wave hello.

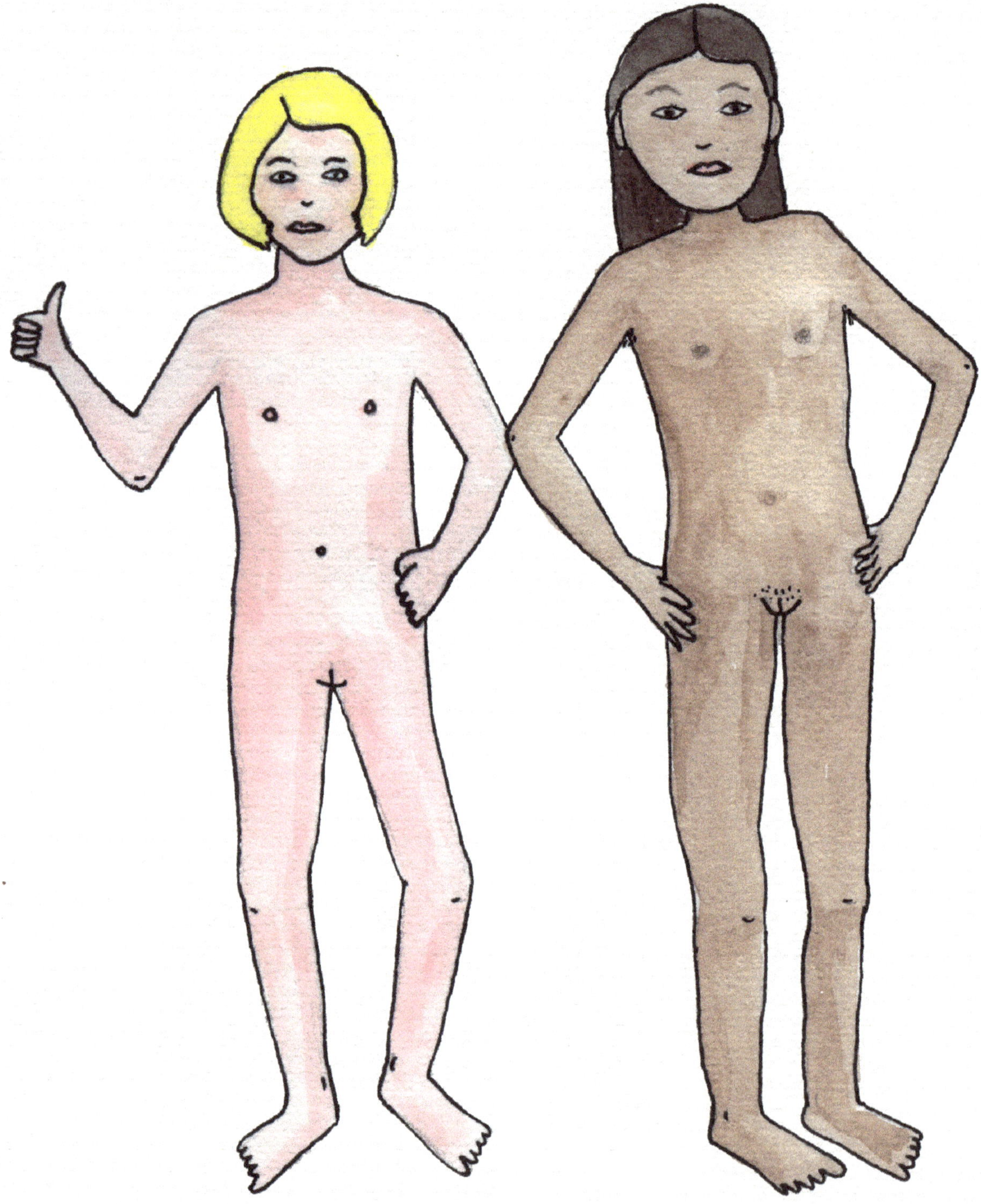

Girls' bodies change as they get older.

They get curvier, grow breast buds and maybe some spots! One breast may grow faster than the other. Some girls will change sooner than the others.

Give me a thumbs up if you are ready to look more closely at the body.

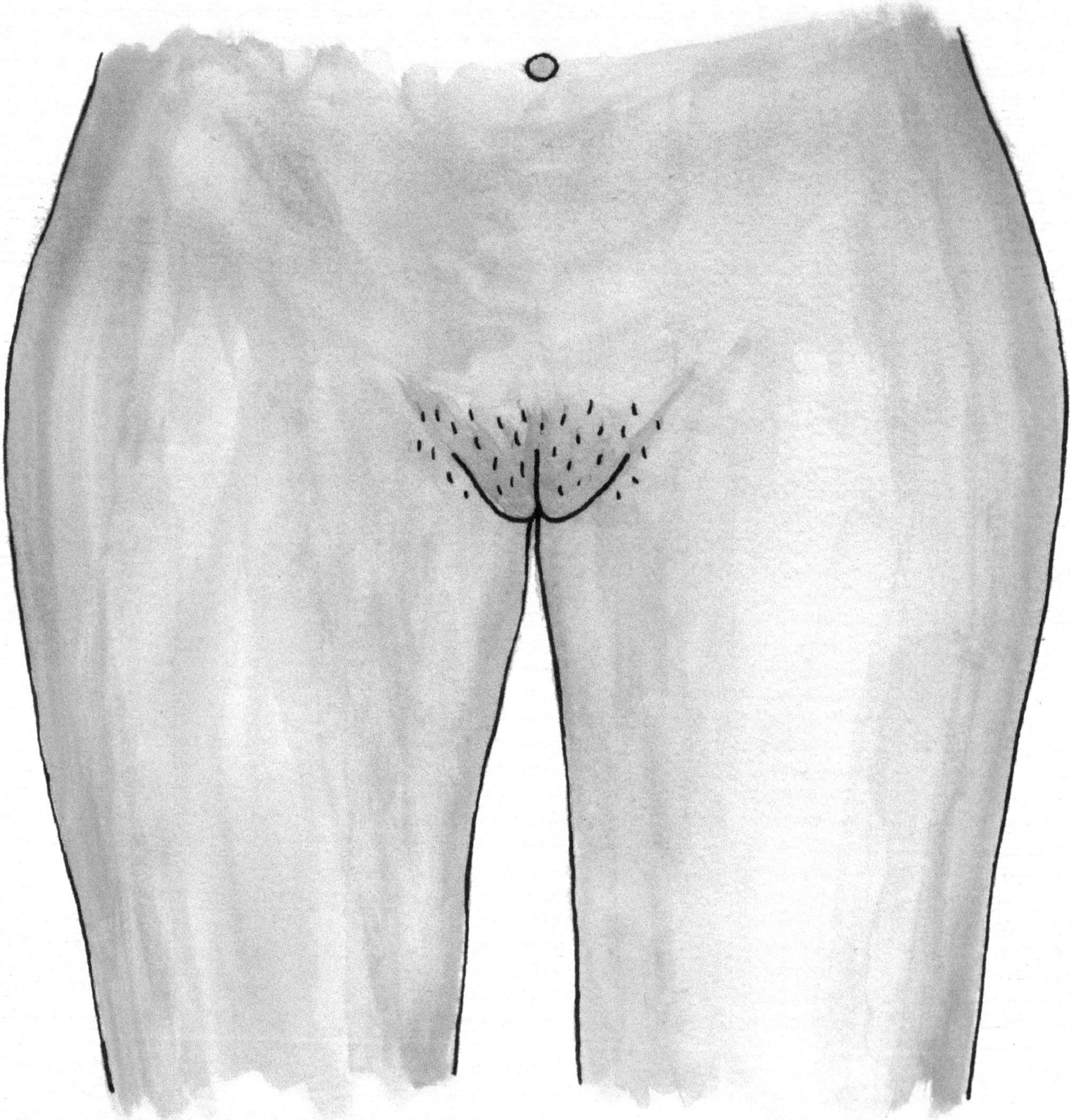

One day you will start to grow pubic hair.

The pubic hair helps protect this special area. When girls are much older, they sometimes choose to have different "hairstyles" there. It's totally YOUR choice if you change it.

Pretend to make a new hairstyle.

Yoni
Vulva

Lady garden
Fanny

Noo noo

FUFU
Privates

Minky

There are lots of names for the area between your legs.

What do you call yours? What's the "proper" name? Do you have a nickname for her?

Say one out loud in your silliest voice.

[The proper term for the area between your legs is vulva.]

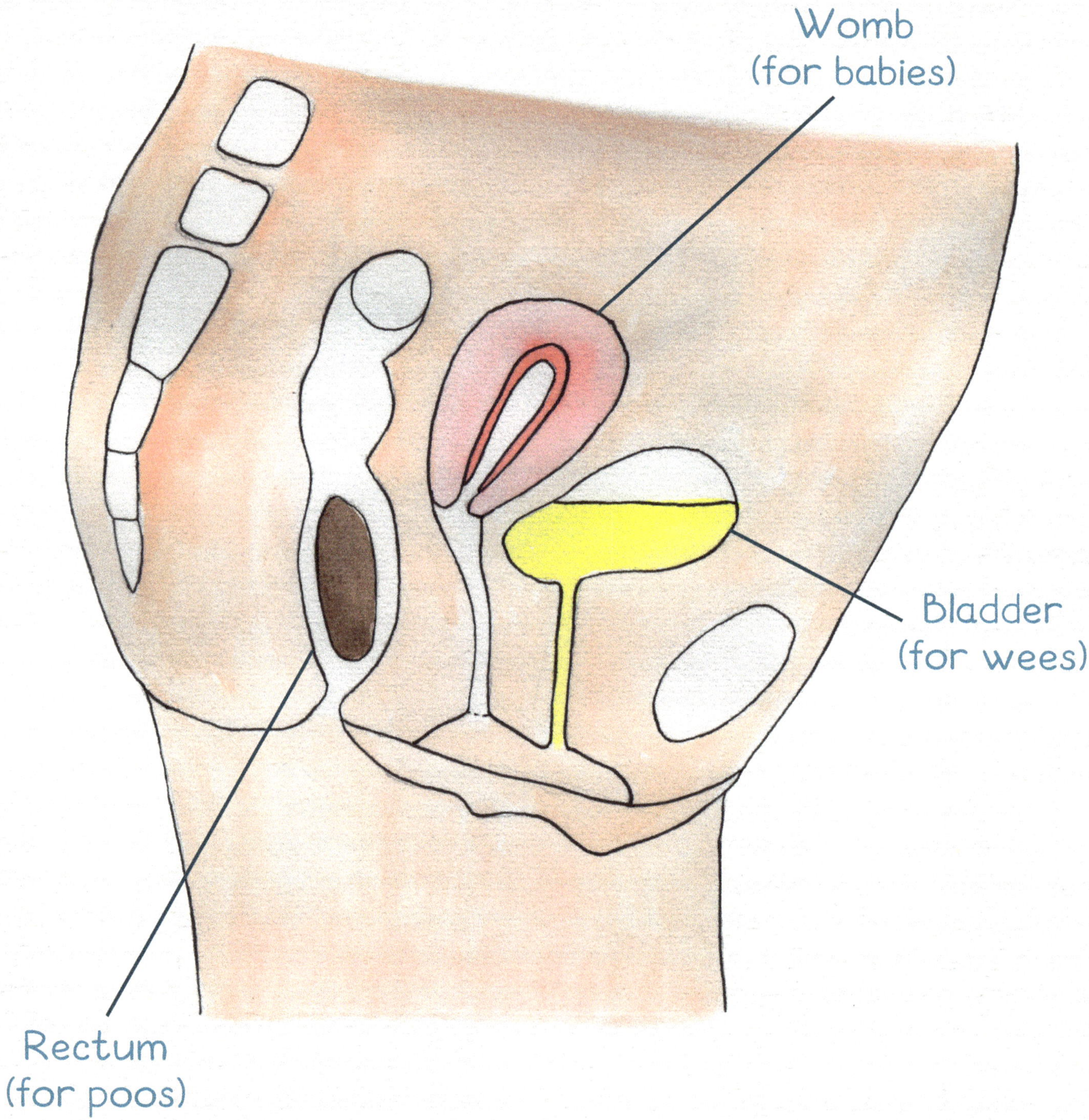
Womb
(for babies)
Bladder
(for wees)
Rectum
(for poos)

You found the three sisters!

The bladder, womb and rectum support each other in the pelvis (the bony part).

Look underneath.

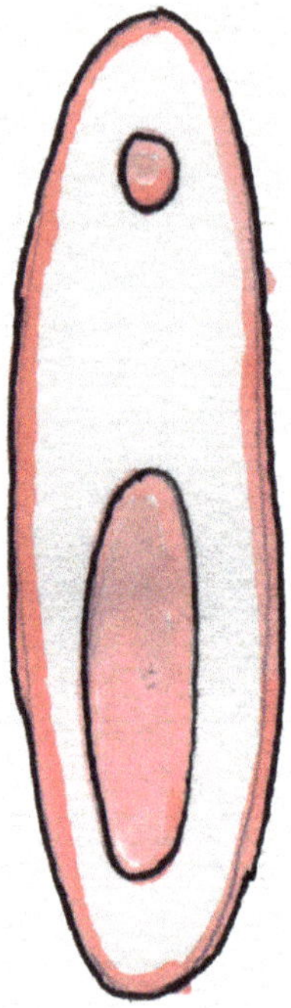

Huh?

What's this all about?

Press gently on each shape.

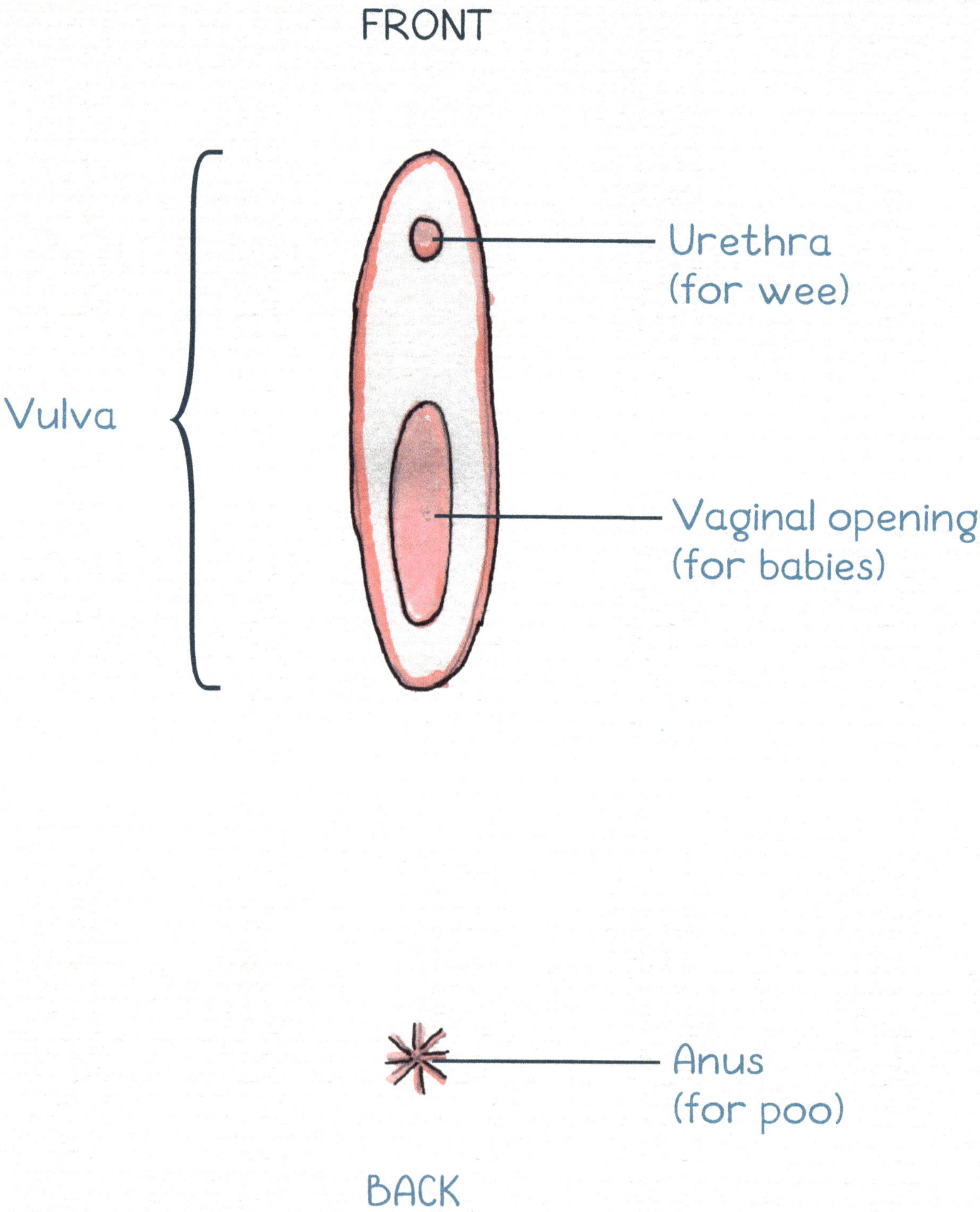
FRONT
Vulva
Urethra
(for wee)
Vaginal opening
(for babies)
Anus
(for poo)
BACK

Oh right! There are three holes underneath a girl.

The three openings let different things come out of your body.

Wipe from front to back.

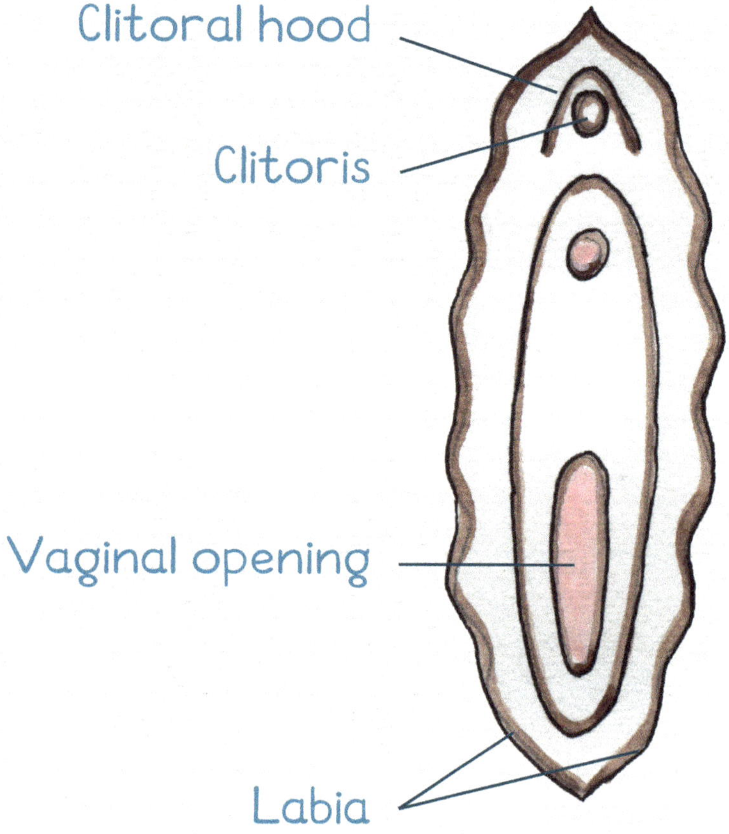
Clitoral hood
Clitoris
Vaginal opening
Labia

You found a real treasure: the clitoris.

The clitoris even has its own hood. Why do you think that is? (More on this later.) You may not be able to see the inner labia yet: they can get bigger as your body starts to change.

Ask "Can I explore the vaginal opening?"

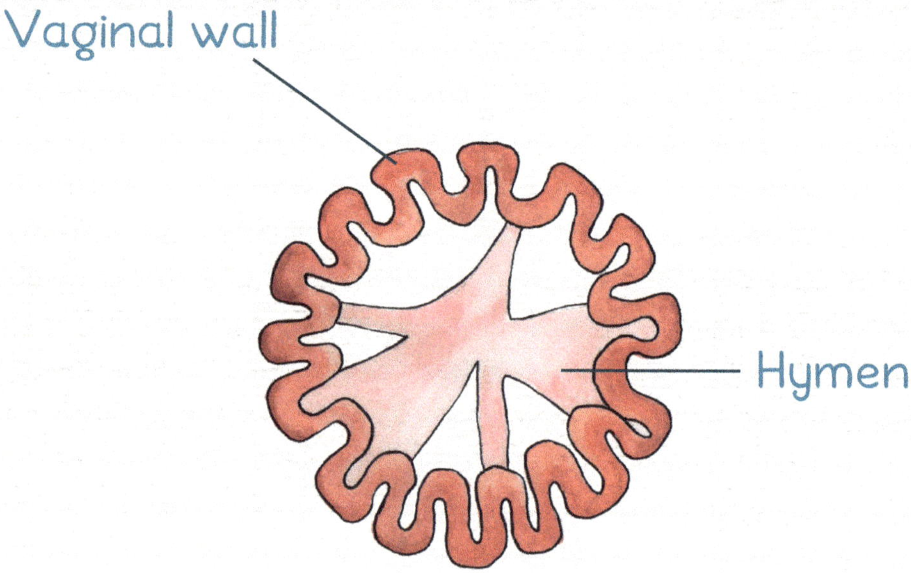
Vaginal wall
Hymen

Hello hymen! What's that? It looks like a hair scrunchy?!

Inside the vaginal opening you may see the hymen. It is also called a vaginal corona (crown). It is often not completely closed but can be stringy or have holes in. One in five girls are born without a hymen that you can see and more lose it naturally.

Place a crown on your head.

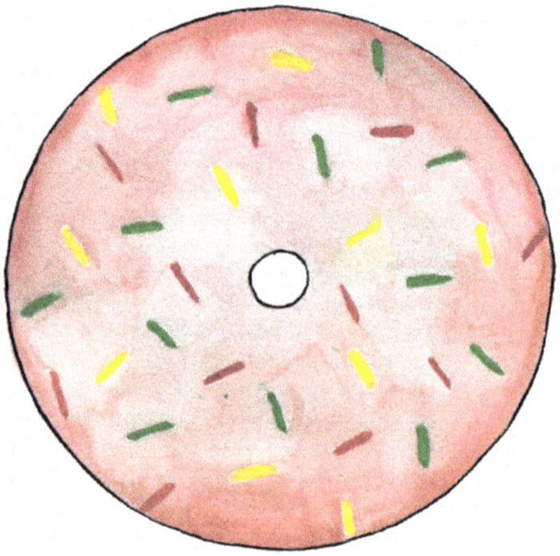

A doughnut? Now this is getting interesting.

Inside the vagina, above the hymen, there is the cervix that looks like a doughnut (but without the sprinkles - the sprinkles are on the picture just for fun!). This is the entrance to the womb. Yes! A womb is where a baby might grow one day.

What flavour doughnut would you eat today?

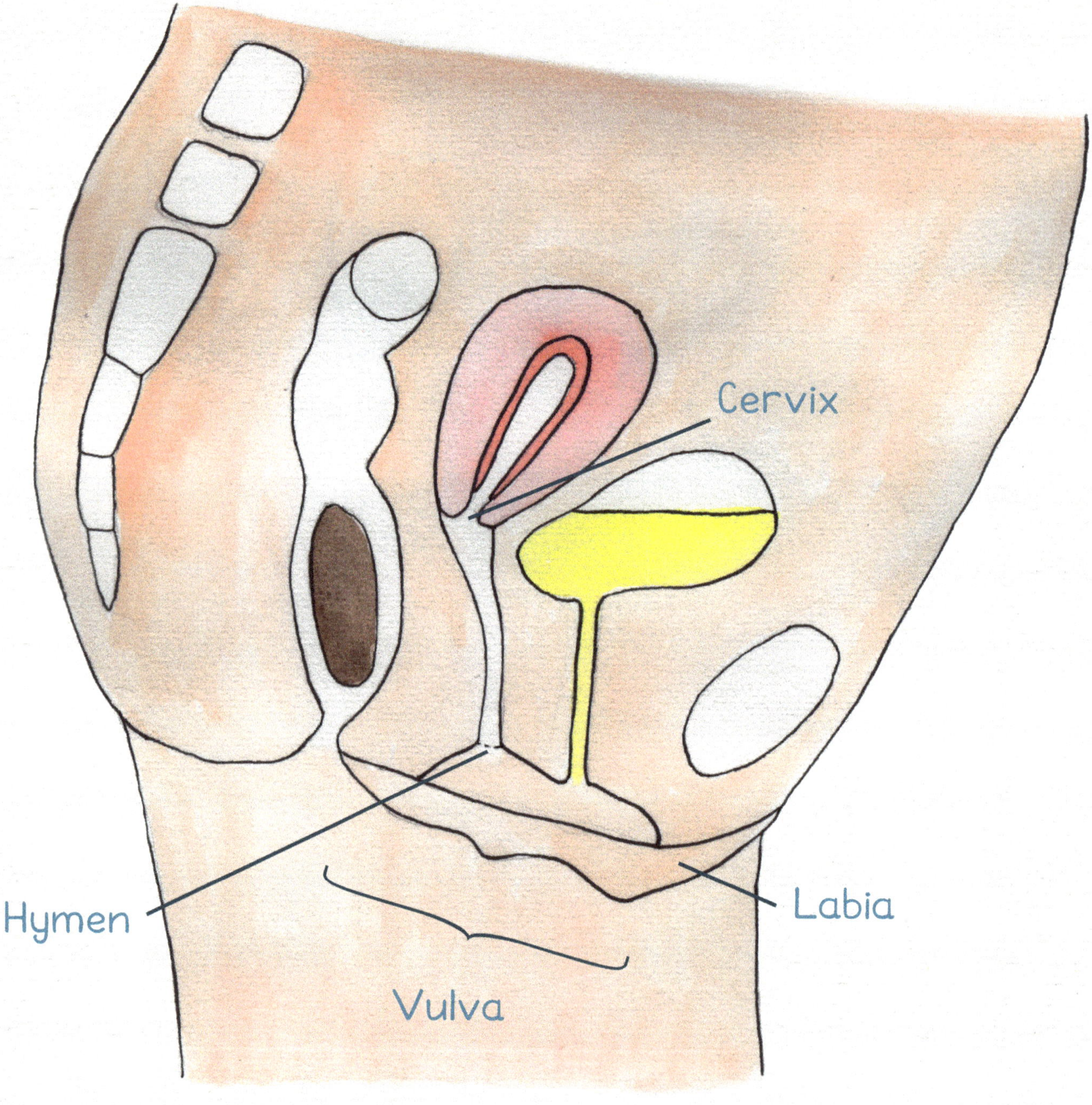
Cervix
Hymen
Labia
Vulva

Let's see how these parts fit together. It's like a jigsaw puzzle.

From the outside we can see the vulva with a mirror. Just inside there might be the hymen. Further up there is the cervix: this can move up and down slightly. The cervix is the opening to, or literally the "neck" of, the womb.

What a lot of words! Which is the hardest to say? Cervix, Hymen or Vulva?

A small pear! This is the size of the womb.

The other name for the womb is uterus. "Womb" is from Old English and "uterus" is Latin. Different words for the same thing!

Push the top of the pear away.

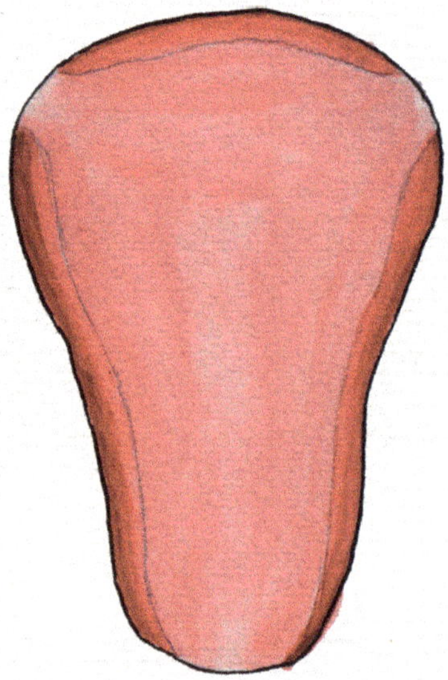

That's better.

The womb is the size of a small upside-down pear in our bodies. It's a red colour because it has a good supply of blood.

Tap the womb two times.

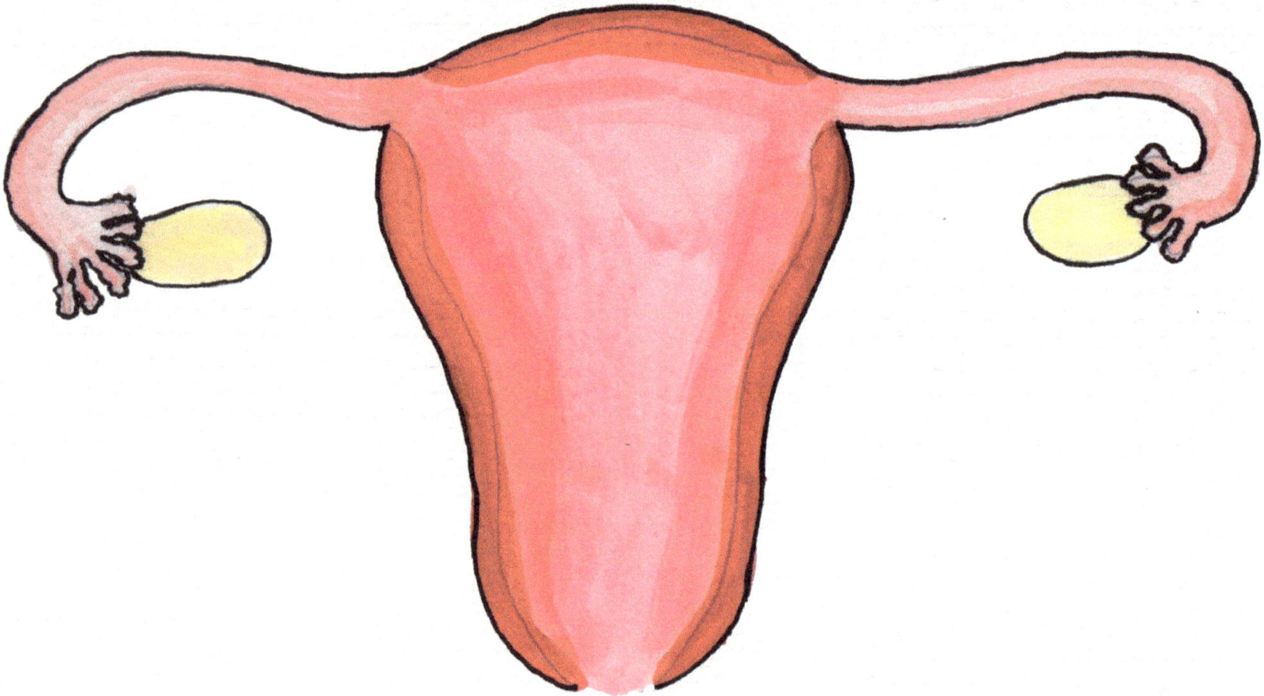

Fabulous Fallopian tubes (or a reindeer?)

The frilly bits at the end of the tubes are called fimbriae and catch the eggs when they are released. "Fimbriae" means a fringe.

Tickle the frilly bits and say "fim-bree-ee!".

What's just happened?

We're inside a female kangaroo! She has two wombs and three vaginas! Can you guess which shapes are the wombs and which the vaginas? (Clue: a vagina leads to a womb.) I'm happy with one of each!

Give me your biggest smile.

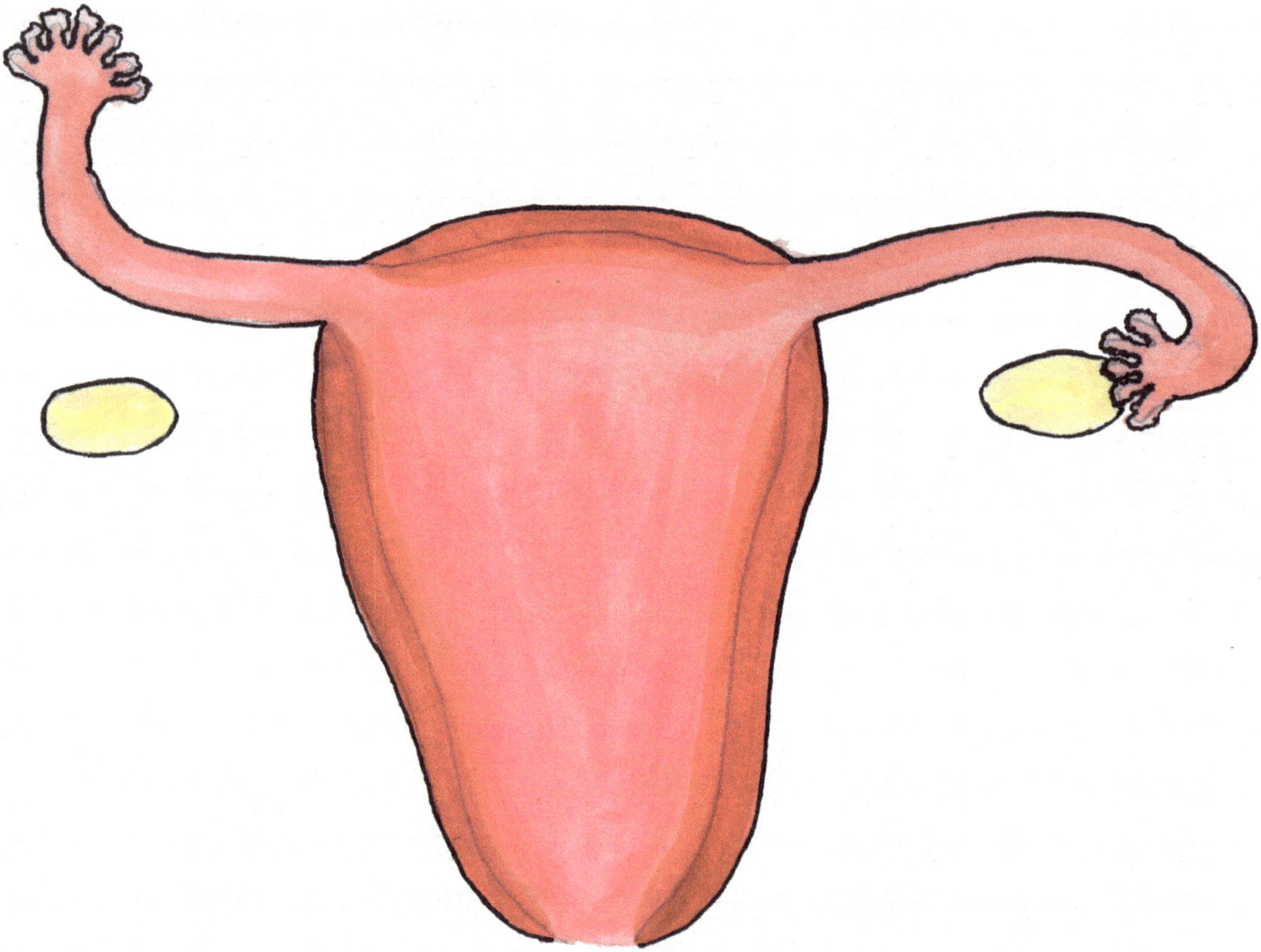

Back to humans. The ovaries are the size of almonds. They are like houses for tiny eggs.

Girls are born with as many as 2 million eggs, but have about 350,000 as a teenager. If one Fallopian tube is blocked the other can pick up eggs from both ovaries.

Tap which ovary you think will release an egg next.

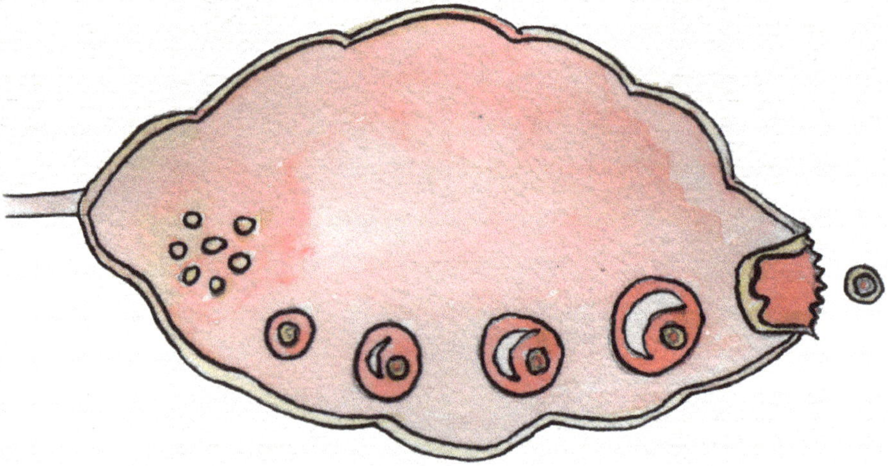

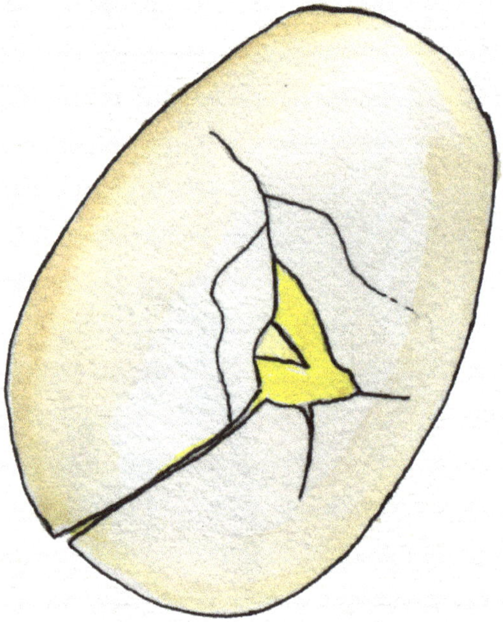

The egg is the only human cell that can be seen with your naked eye (all the others need a microscope).

When you get older, every month or so, an egg will get ready to be released. It bursts out and sometimes you can feel it happen. This is called "mittelschmerz" - a German word because we don't have an English word for it!

Did you know that when your grandma was pregnant with your mum, you already existed as an egg in your mummy's ovary, even though she was just a baby?!

Can you guess which is the human egg?

Now for something else that's magical. The womb can grow in size.

If an egg is picked up by the fimbriae, travels down the Fallopian tube and grows into a baby, the womb changes from the size of a small pear to a grapefruit to a papaya to a large watermelon.

Imagine having a watermelon up your T-shirt!

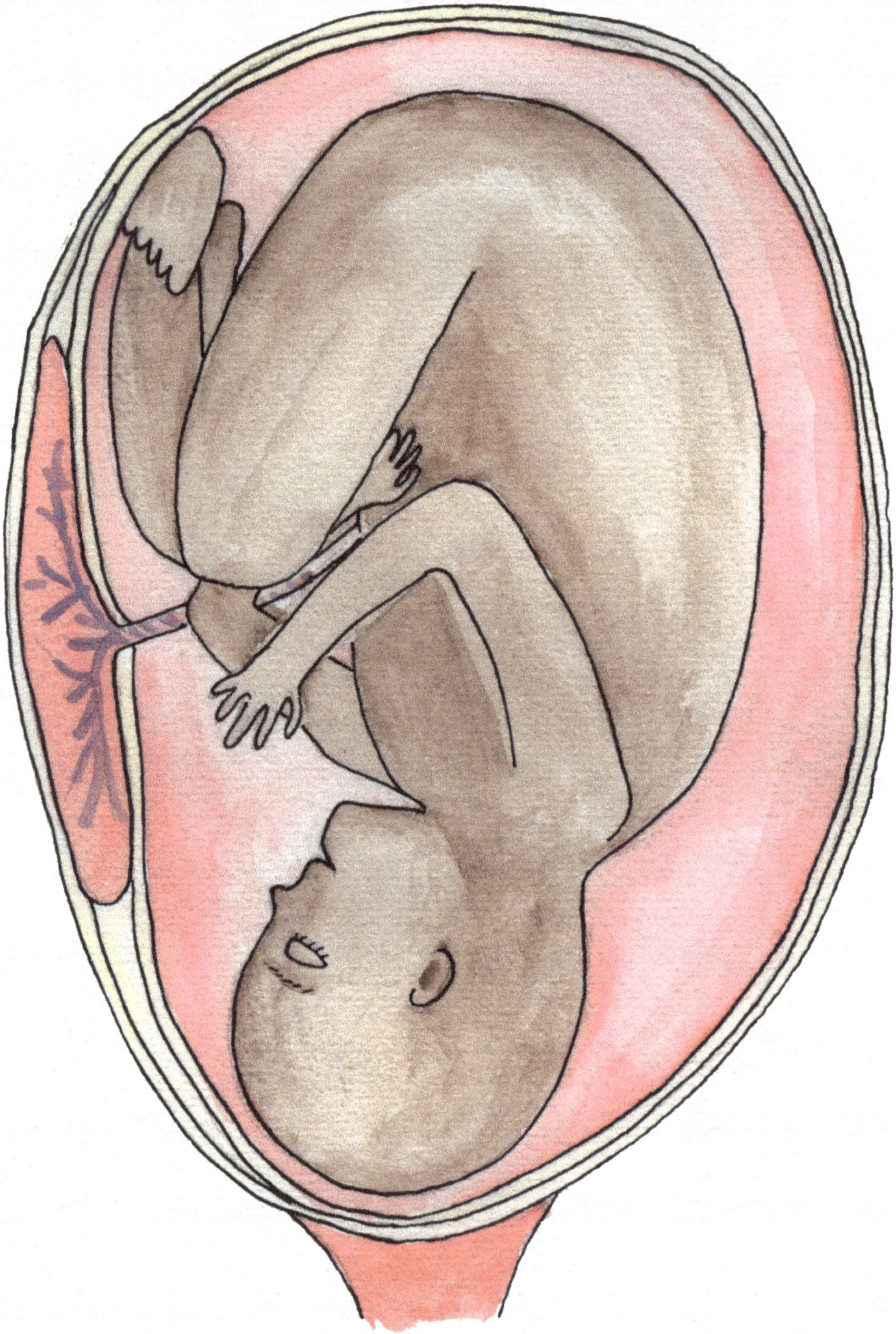

A baby grows in the mummy's womb.

The baby is just the right temperature. The baby is never hungry or thirsty because food is coming through the placenta and the umbilical cord all the time. The sound of the mummy's heartbeat makes the baby feel safe.

Curl up like a baby in a cosy nest.

How does the baby get out?

The amazing cervix is a made a bit like a woven basket that can glide open when it's time for a baby to come out. (Sometimes babies need to come out through the mummy's tummy though.)

Push around the top of the basket just like a baby's head would do.

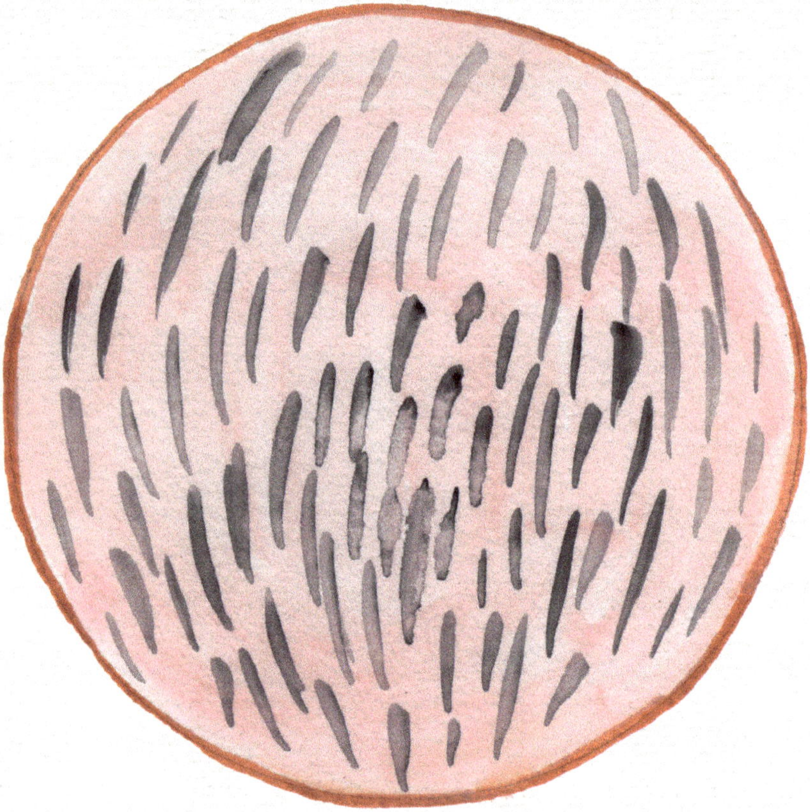

WOW! Can you see the baby's hair?

This is how much room is needed for a baby to come out.
Then the cervix shrinks back.

Yawn as wide as you can.

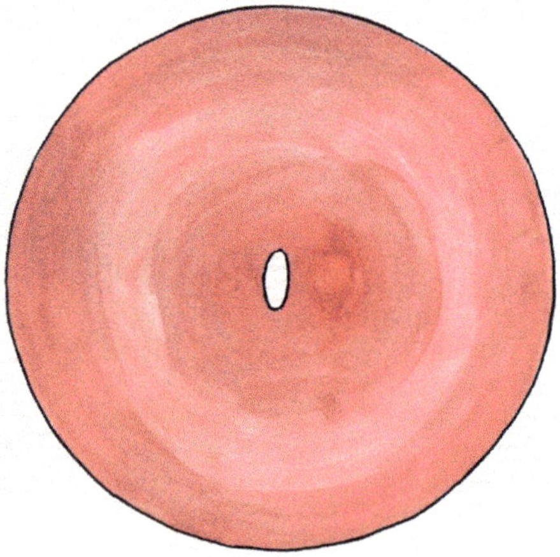

How magically the cervix changes back after the baby comes out!

The hole is tiny again, but is now slit-shaped like a post box!

Pretend to post a teeny-tiny letter.

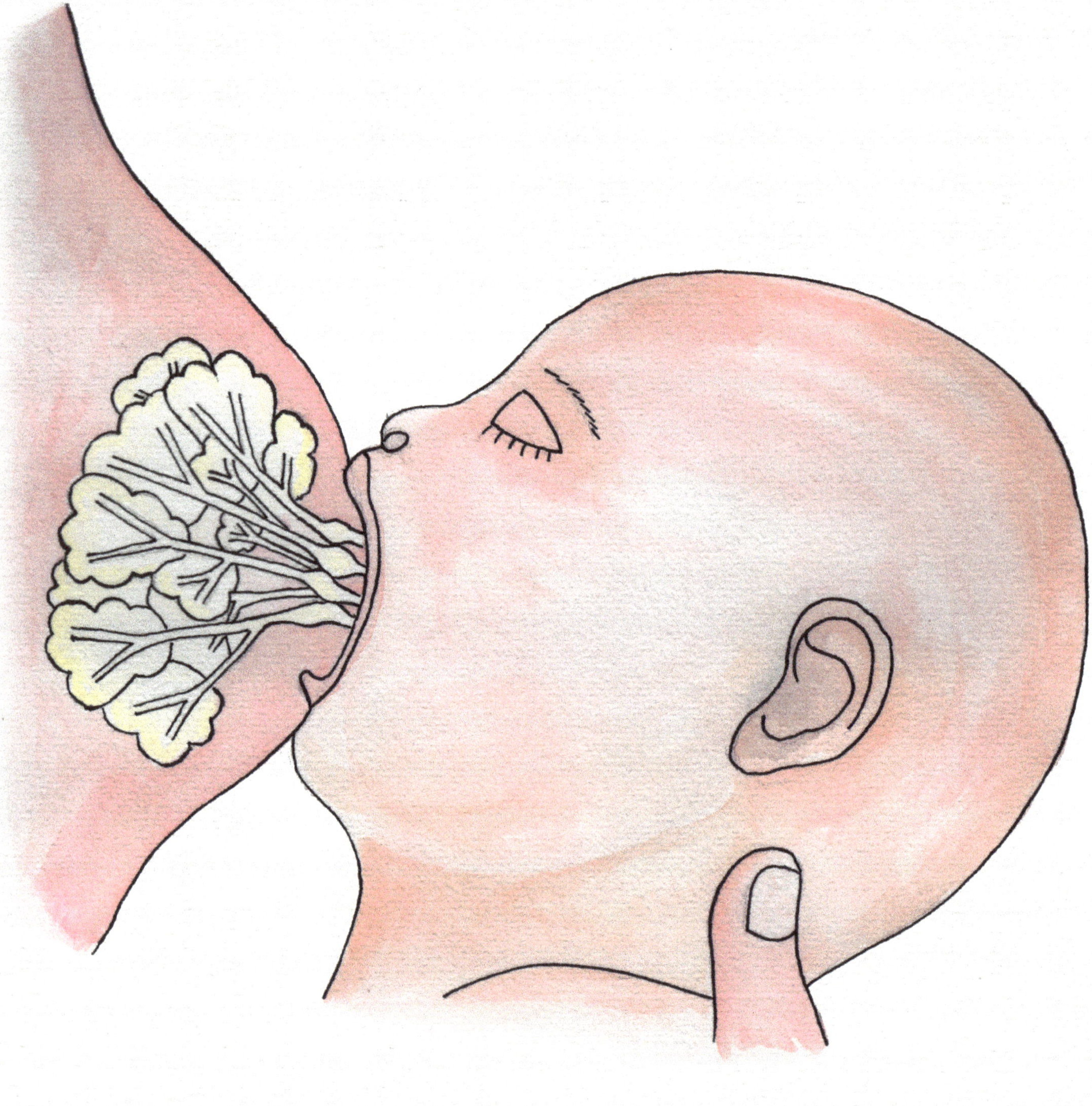

Babies can drink milk from the breast.

Breasts get bigger when the mummy is pregnant, ready for feeding the baby. The milk is made in ducts and comes out of the nipple. There is more than one hole in the nipple. The baby opens his mouth wide and uses his tongue to get the milk out.

Pretend you're licking an ice-cream.

What are we doing outside? Can you say the seasons aloud? Spring, Summer, Autumn and Winter.

We have lots of cycles in life like the cycle of the seasons, cycle of day and night, and the cycle of the moon.

Now go round the circle 12 times for each month of the year. Stop on your favourite season.

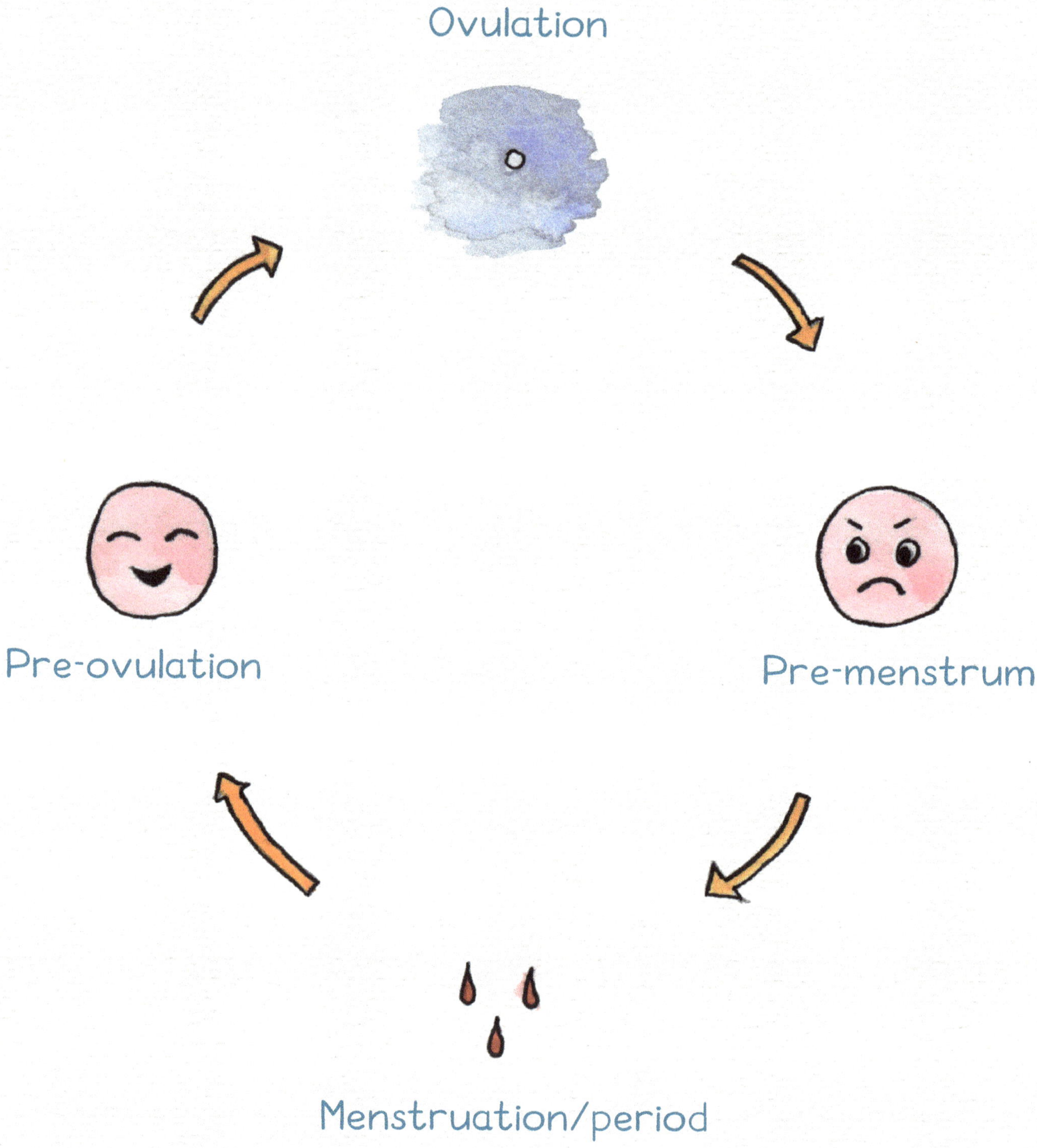
Ovulation
Pre-menstrum
Menstruation/period
Pre-ovulation

Do our bodies cycle? YES!

When we reach puberty the female body changes and how we feel changes over the month. Puberty is when the body starts to practice being able to have a baby.

A girl might feel full of energy when the egg is released (which is called ovulation), but want to rest when she has her period (also called menstruation).

Breathe IN and make an impatient face.
Breathe OUT and make a happy face.

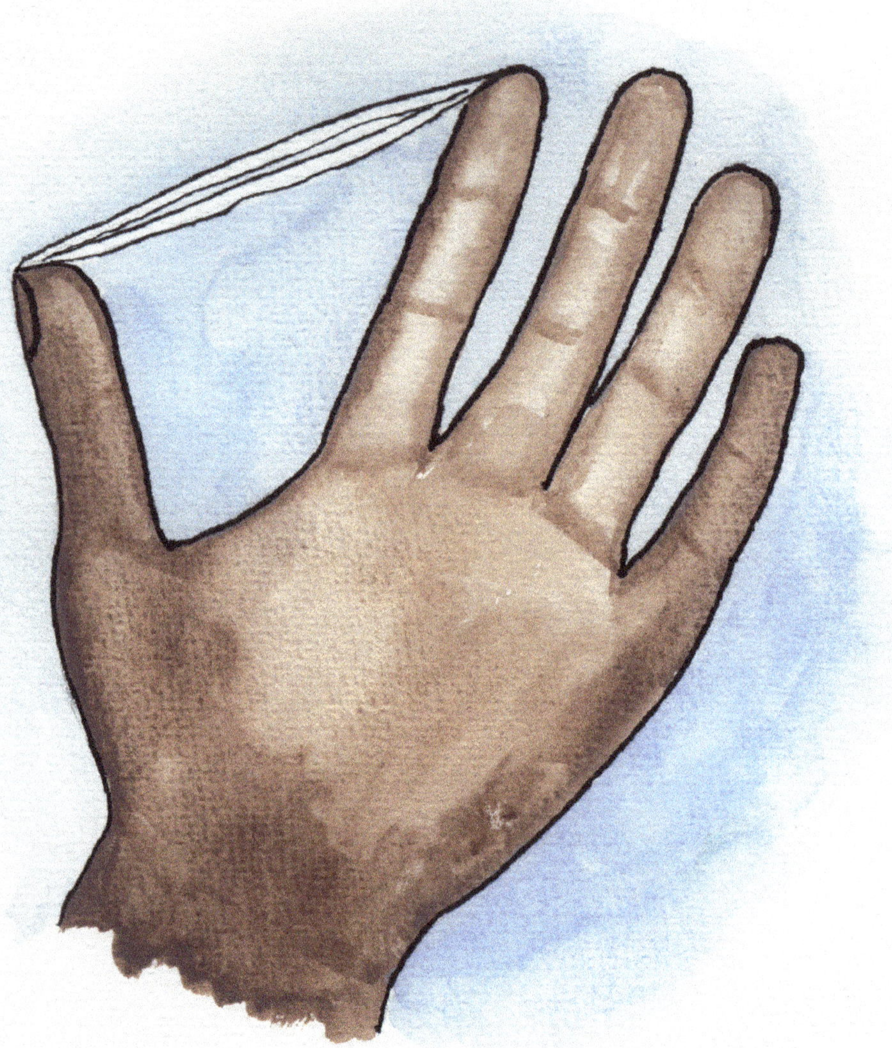

What's that white stuff?

When a girl's body starts to change, she might also find vaginal discharge (also known as cervical mucous) in her knickers around ovulation. This is an amazing slippery, stretchy, useful fluid that's normal to see around the middle of the cycle. In your knickers it might look white, yellowish or even see-through.

Pretend you have a stretchy elastic band around your fingers.

180 ml
160
140
120
100
80
60
40
20

What is a period?

If no baby is made, the egg breaks down and comes out of the body with special blood. This blood contains stem cells that can make anything the body needs, including helping a baby grow.

If there is no baby, the blood is not needed this month. Usually 35-50ml of menstrual blood comes out over 3 to 5 days. Less than a glass of juice at lunchtime! There might be heavier flow for some girls over more days.

Pretend to be a scientist measuring important things.

Auntie Flo

Special time

Moontime

TOM*

Rag week

Menstruation

CRIMSON TIDE

*Time Of the Month

There are lots of name for periods.

Why is it called menstruation? The "men" means month in Latin because periods come monthly. Like in "menarche", which means first month or first period. If you are keeping a diary about your cycle, Day 1 is the first day of your period.

Ask your mum or another person what they call a period.

Disposable or reusable pads
Tampons (also with applicator)
Menstrual cup
Period pants

Will the blood make a mess?

There are lots of ways you can catch the blood. The menstrual blood can be red or brownish. What does your mum or another lady you know use?

Point to the one you would try first.

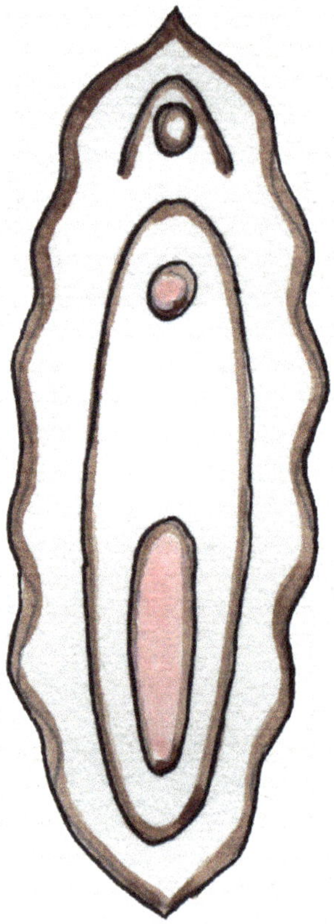

Do you remember the hidden treasure?
The clitoris? Can you point to her now?

We can only see the top of the clitoris when we use a mirror to look between our legs. It has 8000 nerves so is very sensitive and can feel nice for you to touch. She has a hood to protect her.

Your underwear covers your private parts. No-one should ask to see or touch them. Sometimes a doctor, nurse or family member might have to, but they should explain why and ask your permission first.

The most important thing is how YOU feel. Tap the clitoris if you want to.

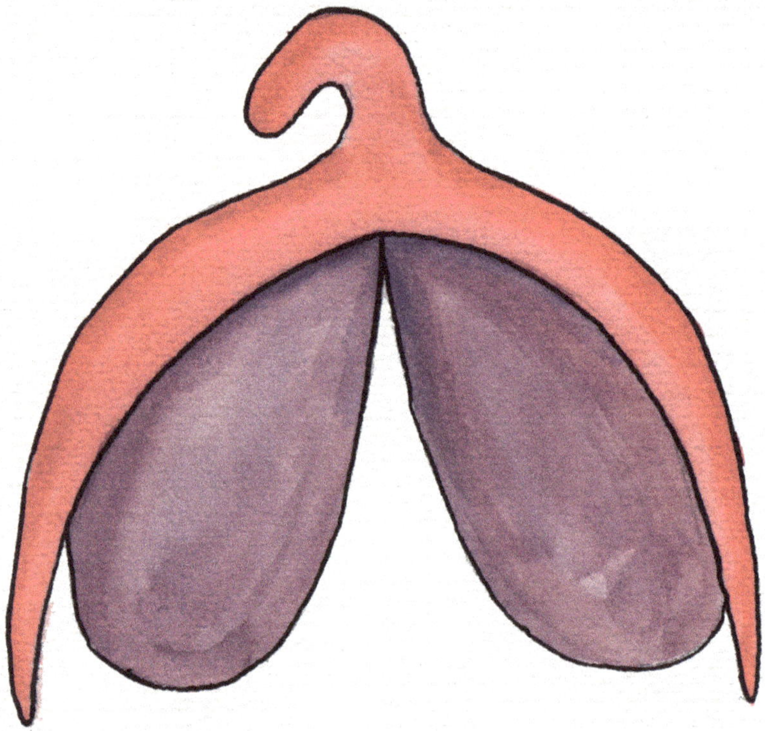

The clitoris looks completely different inside.

The "wings" and bulbs of the clitoris are inside your body. The clitoris can feel nice when touched: you might feel a lovely tingly feeling inside. This whole area of your body is private and special.

She looks a bit like a wishbone. Make a wish right now!

It's time to say goodbye.

I hope you agree that the female body is AMAZING! Lots is hidden, but so many magical changes take place. It might feel strange to think how your body will change so keep talking to your family and friends.

I love my body and I hope you will take good care of yours.

Ruby Luna xx

PS Can you spot 7 differences compared to the Ruby Luna on the first page?

Dear parents/ caregivers. I recommend you encourage looking with a mirror between the legs so she knows what is normal for her and what is where. Perhaps leave a hand mirror in the bathroom.

The question I get from parents and caregivers is when do I start talking about bodies and periods and other things? The answer is from the beginning. Take a deep breath and answer questions as they arise. One sentence usually satisfies curiosity and you don't need to get the answer perfect.

The most important thing is that you are keeping the channels of communication open.

You can find examples of possible questions you may get asked and answers at www.cyclicalwisdom.com/rubyluna, based on my children's questions and those from schools I've visited.

It is normal for cycles to be longer (up to 45 days), irregular and heavier in the first couple of years of having periods while the body adapts to the different levels of hormones.

For my cycle awareness workshops for girls and women, Celebration Days for Girls (10-12 year olds) and retrospective menarche ceremonies for women see

www.cyclicalwisdom.com

For other books and resources, including The Colouring Book for Pregnancy and Birth see

www.tessayoga.co.uk/findoutmore

Published by Castenetto & Co.

Library of Congress cataloguing-in-publication data available.

ISBN 978-0-9933751-2-5

Manufactured & distributed by IngramSpark

Layout and design: Emy Farella

Lightning Source UK Ltd.
Milton Keynes UK
UKHW050245220122
397404UK00002BA/109

9 780993 375125